Library of Davidson College

EARL *PERCY* DINES ABROAD

Hugh, Earl Percy

EARL PERCY
𝔇𝔦𝔫𝔢𝔰 𝔄𝔟𝔯𝔬𝔞𝔡
A Boswellian Episode

By *Harold Murdock*

KENNIKAT PRESS
Port Washington, N. Y./London

KENNIKAT AMERICAN BICENTENNIAL SERIES
Under the General Editorial Supervision of
Dr. Ralph Adams Brown
Professor of History, State University of New York

973.3
M974e

EARL PERCY DINES ABROAD

First published in 1924
Reissued in 1970 by Kennikat Press
Library of Congress Catalog Card No: 72-120886
ISBN 0-8046-1279-X

Manufactured by Taylor Publishing Company   Dallas, Texas

KENNIKAT AMERICAN BICENTENNIAL SERIES

Preface

THE title of this book was suggested by an earlier work, published in 1907, entitled "Earl Percy's Dinner-Table." This was an account of an imaginary dinner given by his Lordship in Boston at the house which he occupied in 1775. The guests, all of my choosing, consisted largely of officers then serving in the garrison, and they discussed such matters as it seemed to me might be of interest to military gentlemen on foreign service.

The present book concerns an actual dinner given in London by General Paoli, the Corsican patriot and refugee, in honor of Earl Percy, on a certain April day in 1778. The reader will note that this dinner was of peculiar interest to Mr. Boswell, who at the time was making his home with General Paoli in London.

To the three guests Boswell mentions as being present at the dinner, I have added four others. Reynolds and Beauclerk fit naturally into any Boswellian group. Hutchinson had a pleasant acquaintance with both Percy and Paoli. No evidence exists of any social intimacy between Pitcairn and the other guests, but, as a prominent London physician, he must have been known to some of these. He certainly knew Reynolds, who painted his portrait,

portrait, and probably Percy, who was an admirer of his brother the Major, killed at Bunker Hill. There is no authority for the implied intimacy between Percy and Beauclerk, but they moved in the same station of life and were fellow members of Brooks's Club.

In the dialogue I have tried to do justice to the known views of the participants on the subjects discussed. In the case of Hutchinson, his sentiments are based upon those recorded in his *Diary* and in his letters, published and unpublished. In some cases phrases, and even sentences, which I have placed in his mouth are taken bodily from these sources. In such instances the passages have been indicated by an asterisk in the text.

Illustrations

Hugh, Earl Percy *Frontispiece*
From a mezzotint by Valentine Green, published January 1, 1777, after a painting presented by the Duke of Northumberland to the Magistrates of Westminster

James Boswell 2
From a contemporaneous painting

General Pasquale Paoli 6
From an engraving by D. Berger, Berlin, 1769

Dr. William Pitcairn 10
From a mezzotint by R. B. Parkes after Reynolds. Reproduced by courtesy of Messrs. Charles E. Lauriat Company

Two Paragraphs from *The New York Gazette and the Weekly Mercury* for May 1, 1775, reporting the Death of Earl Percy at Lexington 16

General James Oglethorpe 20
From a pen-and-ink drawing by Harriet Wilkes

The Rev. Dr. William Dodd 24
From a mezzotint published in London, May 24, 1777

Thomas Hutchinson 30
From the painting by Truman at the Massachusetts Historical Society

Anecdote of Lord Percy 34
From a manuscript in the handwriting of Dr. Percy

Illustrations

"A Sketch of the Action between the British Forces and the American Provincials, on the Heights of the Peninsula of Charlestown, the 17th of June 1775"   38
    From a very rare map published by Jeffreys & Faden in London, August 1, 1775

    Except where otherwise noted the originals of these illustrations are in the possession of the author.

EARL *PERCY* DINES ABROAD

EARL PERCY
Dines Abroad

A Boswellian Episode

EVERY good Boswellian knows that Doctor Thomas Percy gave a dinner to a few friends on Sunday, the 12th of April, 1778.[1] Mr. Boswell, of course, was present, and also Doctor Johnson, Mrs. Anna Williams, and a gentleman who "had recently been admitted into the confidence of" the great ducal family of Northumberland. An unhappy fate decreed that the name of Thomas Pennant, traveller and writer, should be introduced into the conversation that preceded the gathering at the festive board, and Doctor Johnson had not gone far in his praise of him before it became evident that he was commending a person who was cordially hated by his host. Boswell ascribes Percy's animosity to Pennant's lack of appreciation of Alnwick Castle and the Duke of Northumberland's pleasure-grounds appertaining thereto; and, when Doctor Johnson

---

[1] The episode of this dinner, with the resulting complications, appears in Boswell's *Life of Johnson*, ed. 1791, vol. 2, pp. 215–219. Quoted passages are from that edition.

son was fired by contradiction to enlarge his praise, Doctor Percy, without counting the cost, entered the lists in behalf of his noble patron and crossed swords with the mighty sage by whom he would fain have been esteemed.

"I shall record a scene of too much heat between Doctor Johnson and Doctor Percy," writes Boswell, "which I should have suppressed, were it not that it gave occasion to display the truely tender and benevolent heart of Johnson, who as soon as he found a friend was at all hurt by anything which he had 'said in his wrath,' was not only prompt and desirous to be reconciled, but exerted himself to make ample reparation." The din of war and the shouting of the captains may well have alarmed Mrs. Williams, enured as she was to sounds of domestic strife; but the contest ended as suddenly as it had been begun. "PERCY. 'Sir, you may be as rude as you please.' JOHNSON. 'Hold, Sir! Don't talk of rudeness; remember, Sir, you told me' (puffing hard with passion struggling for a vent) 'I was short-sighted. We have done with civility. We are to be as rude as we please.' PERCY. 'Upon my honour, Sir, I did not mean to be uncivil.' JOHNSON. 'I cannot say so, Sir; for I *did* mean to be uncivil, thinking *you* had been uncivil.' Doctor Percy rose, ran up to him, and, taking him by the hand, assured him affectionately that his meaning had been misunderstood; upon which a reconciliation instantly took place."

Boswell assures us that the rest of the evening was pleasant

James Boswell

Dines Abroad

pleasant and gay; but shortly after the affair Percy confided to him that he was still smarting from his wounds. It was all because of that gentleman in the confidence of the Northumberland family, "to whom he [Percy] hoped to appear more respectable, by shewing him how intimate he was with the great Doctor Johnson; and now the gentleman would go away with an impression much to his disadvantage." Not content with these disclosures of the servility of the future Bishop of Dromore, Boswell goes on to say that he was besought by the perturbed divine to lay the whole sad situation before Johnson himself! What could Doctor Johnson do to allay the tortures of Percy's predicament? What he said was, when Boswell presented the matter to him, "This comes of *stratagem;* had he told me that he wished to appear to advantage before that gentleman, he should have been at the top of the house all the time." That Johnson had nothing to suggest is certain beyond a doubt; his antagonist had been gored, a reconciliation had been achieved, and there was "an end on't."

Boswell was in his element. He must have been in the seventh heaven of bliss on realizing his proud status as arbiter and adviser in this silly affair which concerned the personal relations of two distinguished literary men. It was not hard to draw from Johnson some kindly comment upon his late antagonist, and then, with fearful delight, Boswell submitted this scheme to his honest old mentor. "May I be allowed to suggest a mode by which you

you may effectually counteract any unfavourable report of what passed? I will write a letter to you upon the subject of the unlucky contest of that day, and you will be kind enough to put in writing, as an answer to that letter, what you have now said, and in short all that you can say to Doctor Percy's advantage; and as Lord Percy is to dine with us at General Paoli's soon, I will take an opportunity to read the correspondence in his Lordship's presence." Perhaps the Doctor growled and demurred. Here was stratagem with a vengeance; but, in yielding to the wheedling of his friend, he not only impressed Boswell with "his tender and benevolent heart," but secured the inclusion in Boswell's book of that "scene of too much heat," that has been a delight to generations of wondering readers. So Boswell wrote his letter and Johnson's crafty reply was duly received. The Percy of the "Reliques" and the Percies of Northumberland went their way all unconscious of the wiles of the busy little Scotsman in London.

Thus matters stood on the morning of Friday, the 24th of April, 1778. Boswell was abroad at his accustomed hour, and at the Exhibition he chanced to meet Doctor Robertson, the eminent historian. Nothing would do but that he must read Johnson's letter and probably listen as well to a complete recital of all the circumstances that had called it into being. A few hours later, and we can imagine Boswell, properly arrayed for dinner, with the precious missive in his pocket, coming down

Dines Abroad

down the stairs in Paoli's house. Victory was almost within his grasp. Did it occur to him that, after all, the important guest might not appear? A sudden illness or pressing business in the Lords might leave a vacant chair. If he was oppressed by any such misgivings as these, conceive his relief and joy when, on entering the drawing-room, he beheld a young man in the uniform of a general officer standing in conversation with his host.

That Boswell regarded the dinner as a triumph is evidenced by the note which he wrote to Doctor Percy on the day following the event. It is not clear why he should have written, as it appears from his narrative that he managed to breakfast with the Doctor on the same morning and informed him verbally of his scheme and its happy success. "He thanked me in the warmest terms," says Boswell, "and was highly delighted with Doctor Johnson's letter in his praise, of which I gave him a copy. He said, 'I would rather have this than degrees from all the Universities in Europe. It will be for me, and my children and grandchildren.'"

One other incident and the episode is closed. Here it is in Boswell's words: "Doctor Johnson having afterwards asked me if I had given him a copy of it, and being told I had, was offended, and insisted that I should get it back, which I did."

Imagine the sensations of Percy when, as Bishop of Dromore in 1791, he found this story set forth at length in Boswell's immortal book! He had been apprehensive

as

as to Boswell's intentions and had striven vainly to extract from him a promise that his name should be rigidly excluded from his book. He must have winced at being made ridiculous by a man whom he had come to regard as little better than an infamous scribbler; and yet he may have been painfully aware that this same scribbler had not seriously transgressed the truth. Certain changes in the narrative, a studied softening of phrases, were conceded by the author in his second edition of the "Life"; but there was no retraction, and for more than a century the episode has stood in literature as we have just reviewed it. There is the record of how Percy lost his temper, his self-respect, his copy of Johnson's letter, and, so far as Boswell could achieve it, his claim to be regarded as a devout and unworldly Right Reverend Father in God.

Who thinks to-day of criticising the unique Boswell for his transgression of the laws of friendship and good taste in this affair? Our real grievance against him lies in the fact that, despite the meticulous character of his narrative, he has failed to include the story of Paoli's dinner. All he tells us is that there were present, besides the host and himself, General Oglethorpe, Lord Percy, and some others. Who were those other guests? Was there good talk? Did Boswell present "the correspondence" as alleged in his book, or did he merely read the Doctor's letter? How did Earl Percy receive the carefully prepared communication? Here is a lapse indeed. Paoli is as silent as

General Pasquale Paoli

Dines Abroad

as Boswell, and no hint has come down to us from the other guests. Where facts fail, we must have recourse to fancy. If our curiosity is keen and our imagination strong, we may yet travel back over that long road to 1778, and find ourselves in South Audley Street in the days when George III was King.

A room panelled in deal, a glitter of candles on table and wall, a cheerful fire sputtering and crackling in the iron grate. Dinner is over, but the guests linger at their wine. A peal of laughter greets the trenchant sally of the Honourable Topham Beauclerk.[1] Doctor William Pitcairn,[2] President of the Royal College of Physicians, alone seems unmoved by the merriment as he peruses a paper that a servant has placed in his hands. Mr. Boswell's flushed face bears unmistakable signs of perturbation. General Paoli smiles broadly as he glances from Boswell to Beauclerk. Shaking his forefinger at the former, he delivers himself of the following declamation: "Ah, my dear Sir, do you remember when you came to my country and fetched me some letter recommending you? But I was of the belief you might be an impostor, and I supposed in my mind you was an espy; for I look away from you, and in a moment I look to you again, and I behold your tablets. Oh! You was to the work of writing down all I say! Indeed I was angry. But soon I discover you was no impostor and no espy; and

[1] See Note 1.
[2] See Note 2.

and I only find I was the monster you had come to discern.[1] I was indeed angry, but Mr. Beauclerk, he is playful."

"Beauclerk is playful," murmured Earl Percy as he arranged paper and ink upon the table. "Even Mr. Boswell must admit that he has a damned pleasant way of saying anything that he hopes will give offence. For myself, I feel assured that Mr. Boswell will pursue no course that would bring me before a court-martial or secure for my friend Governor Hutchinson a verbal coat of tar and feathers from his indignant countrymen."

"But, General — gentlemen," expostulated Boswell, "I have no note-book, I have no tablets. This is a letter" — displaying it with its broken seal — "a letter from a distinguished friend whom we all know and respect, concerning a gentleman in whom Lord Percy takes an interest and which I thought his Lordship—"

"Ah," interrupted Beauclerk, "we must, of course, make way for Lord Percy's friends."

At this moment of Boswell's opportunity, General Paoli, who was assisting Percy in his preparations, became conscious that Doctor Pitcairn was at his side, tendering regrets and apologies for his early departure. "I am heartily sorry, General, but Doctor Heberden's chaise is at the door and I must obey a call that brooks of no delay. My life is full of interruptions, and I wish that

---

[1] This passage is taken from what Paoli said to Miss Burney of Boswell. See *Diary and Letters of Madame D'Arblay*, Austin Dobson's edition, London, 1904, vol. 2, p. 100.

Dines Abroad

that I might have had this evening to enjoy this good company to the full." Then, turning to Earl Percy who had risen from his chair, he spoke with visible emotion of the comfort and gratification it had given him to hear his deceased brother so warmly commended by his commanding officer, to hear how much he had been esteemed in the last days of his life, not only in the army, but among the poor infatuated people of the Province for whose real interests he had laid down his life. "The respect paid to his memory by His Majesty's Government," continued the Doctor, "is most grateful to me and to his bereaved family, but your generous praise of one whom you are pleased to style a comrade and friend is a real solace, that I shall try to communicate to those whose affliction is even deeper than mine."

"What I have said, Doctor," replied Percy, "was said honestly and from the heart"; and then, as Pitcairn took his leave, he called after him, to say, "Remember, please, my compliments to Doctor David[1] and I am to see him at Northumberland House on my return from the North."

The door closed behind the departing guest. The company returned to their seats. Percy dipped his pen in ink and Paoli drew up a chair to watch him at his task. Thomas Hutchinson, late Captain General and Governor in Chief of His Majesty's Province of Massachusetts Bay, moved quietly across the room and stood by

[1] See Note 2.

by Percy's side. Mr. Boswell felt that his chance had come. He drew his letter from his pocket and refilled his glass. At this time he was "a water-drinker upon trial by Doctor Johnson's recommendation," but he felt that circumstances altered cases. "Now, Bozzy," said Beauclerk. "Ah," remarked Percy, "now we will hear of my unnamed friend."

But at this moment the door opened and there reappeared the portly form and kindly face of Doctor Pitcairn, hat in hand, his cloak upon his arm. "My apologies, gentlemen, but I have left my cane. Pray don't rise; I see it by my chair. It is rather a famous cane and I assure you a troublesome one. Holding it in trust for my successor, I keep it always by me. City doctors do not wear swords, but for my peace of mind I should have a belt and scabbard." "The gold-headed cane!" exclaimed Beauclerk with visible interest. " I have heard of it from Doctor Warren. Pray tell us, Doctor, who owned it in Queen Elizabeth's time."

"What is this?" queried Boswell, his curiosity aroused.

"Pardon my haste, gentlemen," replied Pitcairn. "I think Sir Joshua can give you the story. Good night!"[1]

Topham Beauclerk turned to Reynolds and informed him of Pitcairn's parting message. Mr. Boswell, though curious, was painfully conscious of hope deferred. The artist sipped his wine and explained that all he knew of the cane he learned from Doctor Pitcairn a year or two before,

[1] See Note 3.

Dr. William Pitcairn

before, when he was painting his portrait. It was Doctor Radcliffe's property in King William's time and from him passed to Doctor Mead who practised in Queen Anne's day. Doctor Askew had it from Mead, and he bequeathed it to Pitcairn, who hoped that his nephew would fulfil his present promise and succeed him in the title.

OGLETHORPE. "I can recall, as a boy, having old Radcliffe pointed out to me. Was he not an eccentric, contentious man whose skill was doubted in many quarters?" BEAUCLERK. "Every physician is doubted in some quarters. Radcliffe was honest and courageous if the legend be true that he told King William he would not for his three kingdoms have his two legs." BOSWELL. "Doctor Mead was not only a great physician, but a patron of the arts whose opinion and influence were much valued. He had a fine library, not the equal of Mr. Beauclerk's, but it was sold for more than five thousand pounds." REYNOLDS. "Radcliffe was a good friend of Sir Godfrey Kneller of my profession. They were neighbours and their grounds adjoined, being divided by a wall in which there was a door. The story is that, Radcliffe's servants having plundered Sir Godfrey's gardens, he sent an angry message to his friend threatening to close the door. Radcliffe replied that he might do anything he pleased with it except paint it, to which Kneller responded, in better humour, 'I can take anything from him but physic.'"

Sir

Sir Joshua was evidently pleased with his story, and with the laughter it created. Then Earl Percy rose, smoothed his paper upon the table, and addressed his host. "Here, General, is the problem and you can answer your own question. I hope General Oglethorpe [1] will give us his opinion. Here is Boston with its garrison. This is the Charles River, that the rebel redoubt, with these fences and walls extending down to the Mystic. This is the village of Charlestown that was burned."

Hutchinson interrupted to say that it was an ancient and thriving village and to ask if his Lordship regarded its destruction as an act of military necessity. "I have no doubt that it was," replied Percy. "Howe was annoyed by musketry from the houses. I believe it was a pretty place. I visited it but once, and that by moonlight."[2] Then, returning to his map, he continued to address Paoli. "The neck is here very narrow with a causeway sometimes flooded by the tides, and in this direction lies Cambridge where the college is and where the rebel headquarters was established. The redoubt was thrown up in one night, and, properly manned by artillery, would have commanded the town. Had you been in command at Boston, how would you have acted in the crisis?" Paoli studied the sketch. "Is this a river?" he queried. Earl Percy laughed. "Yes, Sir, that is the Mystic River and this is the Charles. Charlestown lies a
peninsula

[1] See Note 4.
[2] See Note 5.

peninsula between the two, connected with the mainland by this narrow neck. I am sorry I am so bad a draughtsman." Then, turning to Beauclerk, "Lady Di would have done this better."[1]

Beauclerk murmured something in Reynolds's ear which caused the artist to smile and stroll over to where Percy was standing. "A very clever piece of work," he said, as he adjusted his spectacles and surveyed the sketch, "but what is it? I see a map, a plan. Now which is land and which is water?" Percy laughed again and suggested that Sir Joshua might help him out, as he was neither artist, draughtsman, nor engineer. "What do these lines represent?" asked Reynolds. "High land, Sir," explained Percy; "Charlestown Heights, of which our two generals here are to dispossess the enemy." REYNOLDS. "May I use your pen? Hold, I have my pencils, I am never without them." Then, seating himself at the table, with all the guests about him, the great and fashionable artist of the day, with a few strokes and tints, created land, water, and elevations with a clearness that was unmistakable even to old Oglethorpe's failing sight. "Marvellous!" said Percy. "Sir Joshua has dispensed with the necessity for Lady Di."

Mr. Boswell, torn betwixt enthusiasm and anxiety, could not refrain at this moment from drawing Mr. Hutchinson aside to whisper in his ear, "What an experience, Sir, to see the great Paoli, the famous Sir Joshua

[1] See Note 1.

Joshua Reynolds, and a distinguished field officer who has the blood of Hotspur in his veins, grouped in this casual and unstudied intimacy! Do you not share with me the exhilaration that comes from such associations and find delight in playing your part in the great world of London?"

Hutchinson smiled and replied simply, "I am fond of London, and my London friends." Then, addressing Earl Percy, he spoke of Mr. Pelham's map of Boston and its environs, published in London within the year. His Lordship had not seen the map, but remembered Mr. Pelham in Boston when he was seeking permission from Headquarters to make his surveys on the Charlestown peninsula. "I am afraid that he was at first regarded as a spy or a person of doubtful friendship to government. I heard him much commended later. I am glad he carried his enterprise through to success. Is his map a creditable piece of work, Sir, — you know the country?" HUTCHINSON. "I do know the country and regard the map as excellent. It is on a large scale and even private houses are marked on it. Many an evening have I pored over it and in imagination travelled the well-known streets and roads in company with old friends and neighbours. My family do not encourage my affection for Mr. Pelham's work. They fear that it depresses my spirits. I understand that Pelham is now in town and can be found at Mr. Copley's." REYNOLDS. "Who spoke of Copley?" HUTCHINSON. "I was saying, Sir Joshua, that a townsman

Dines Abroad

a townsman of mine, Mr. Henry Pelham,[1] is now staying with Mr. Copley the artist. They are half brothers, I think." REYNOLDS. "Copley is a good man, Sir, and an excellent painter. Have you heard that he is deeply moved by the dramatic incident of Lord Chatham's seizure last month?[2] He is much impressed by the scene and I think he will re-create it upon canvas. It is a subject quite to his taste and he will handle it nobly." HUTCHINSON. "What is the latest news from Chatham?" REYNOLDS. "Doctor Pitcairn was saying that he is beyond the help of medical skill." BEAUCLERK. "The talk at Brooks's this afternoon was that he fails from day to day. Pitt has left to join his regiment at Gibraltar.[3] The old man was as insistent for this as he was against his serving in America."

There was more talk of Chatham while the two generals pored over their map, exchanging comments with each other. The conversation ceased as Percy said, "Now, gentlemen, will you order the attack?"

Paoli was the first to speak. "Why should we attack at all? What say you, Oglethorpe? How would Prince Eugene have proceeded in this matter?" "The Prince was too great a soldier for me to interpret," replied the other, "but I agree with you, Sir, that to attack would be monstrous. We have closed the neck by the fire of the ships

---
[1] See Note 6.
[2] Not strictly correct. Chatham was stricken in the House of Lords on April 7.
[3] See Note 7.

ships; can we not bring another up the Mystic and cannonade their flank and rear? Is it not possible to make a landing at the neck and gain the high land behind the rebel works?" "Ah," said Percy, "I heard those questions asked in Boston!"[1]

His Lordship continued: "There were no serious difficulties attending this plan, but you are well aware, General, of the technical objections that could be urged to placing a force between the rebel entrenchments on the one hand and their main body on the other. The truth is, I think, that when Howe crossed the Charles, he did not know that the country people had extended their works to the Mystic. This was a late enterprise of theirs, performed with prodigious speed. Perhaps it was too late then to have towed heavy guns up the stream to the point you have indicated, but it is certain that Howe met the crisis by asking for reënforcements and not for ships. He tried their flank, but found them prepared and the water flooding the Mystic Beach. Failing here, he felt he had the choice of returning to his boats or storming the lines in his front." BEAUCLERK. "I understand that our artillery was thwarted by the wiles of a pretty woman.[2] George Selwyn says—" PERCY. "Gossip, Sir, arrant gossip, despite the excellence of your authority. It was the devil himself who balked our six-pounders, though they saved the day at last." OGLETHORPE. "You say our army was cut to pieces." PERCY. "Four out of every

[1] See Note 8.
[2] See Note 9.

Night put an end to the Firing, but the Country having been alarmed, the Provincials poured in from every Quarter. When the Exprefs left the Place, he fays there could not be lefs than 30 or 40,000 of our Men under Arms, and more coming very faft. They had furrounded the Regular Troops, and were throwing up Entrenchments to hinder their Retreat on N. E. Side, where a Ship of War lies within a Mile of them. Our Men are in high Spirits, no dejected countenances among them, which is not the cafe with the Regulars. It is fuppofed that about 150 of the latter are Killed, and among them Lord Percy and General Haldimand, but this is only conjecture. Of our Men it is fuppofed we have Loft about 30 or 40, but none of Note, that we can hear of. The whole Colony is alarmed, and has already Marched, or is ready.

This moment an Exprefs is arrived. The Troops Encamped on Thurfday Night got into Bofton under the Guns of the Ships. The report of General Haldimand's Death is confirmed. Piercy is Miffing, fuppofed to be Burned with the other Dead, by the Regular Troops in a Barn. Col. Murray's Son, who was their Pilot out, is Dead.

From 'The New York Gazette and the Weekly Mercury,' May 1, 1775

every ten men we put in the field were hit. Nearly one hundred officers fell." OGLETHORPE. "Monstrous! I think I read that your Lordship narrowly escaped with your life." PERCY. "No, General, I was snugly tucked away out of danger, and only a part of my brigade was engaged. In these days one need not be surprised at anything that appears concerning his life or death. I recall reading in American newspapers circumstantial accounts of how I had been killed in the affair of Lexington."

A smile flickered for an instant on Beauclerk's impassive face as he drawled out, "Lexington! I have heard of that. Oh! where they

> "Taught Percy fashionable races
> And modern modes of Chevy Chaces." [1]

To which Percy replied, "You are exactness itself, Beauclerk. Will you have the rest?

> "Whence Gage extols from gen'ral hearsay,
> The great activ'ty of Lord Piercy;
> Whose brave example led them on,
> And spirited the troops to run;
> And now may boast at royal levees
> A Yanky-chace worth forty Chevys." [2]

BEAUCLERK. "Egad, but your Lordship is familiar with the very latest word in your praise." PERCY. "I studied those lines in America and received promptly on my landing in England a copy of the London reprint from the

[1] Trumbull's *McFingal*, ed. 1775, p. 1.
[2] *Ibid.*, p. 37.

the friendly hand of Charles Fox." Boswell. "And who is this scurrilous scribbler who would have us know that he reads 'Hudibras'?" Percy. "A rather clever fellow, I should say. Who is he, Governor? Mr. Boswell is interested." Hutchinson. "Mr. Trumbull is a young man of singular talent. He belongs to Connecticut, but has spent some time in Boston. He was admitted to Yale College at seven years of age, but his parents wisely delayed his entrance until he had passed his thirteenth birthday. He has become a satirist who favors the popular cause without altogether admiring it. He is a witty foe of Government, but none the less dangerous for that."[1]

Mr. Boswell was far from his goal. He had listened patiently to what he regarded as quite irrelevant to the subject of the evening. In his heart he wished that America had never been discovered, or, at all events, that the Battle of Bunker Hill had never been fought. He saw, however, a glimmer of hope. It was a long shot, but worth the trying. "The man seems familiar with the ballad of Chevy Chace," he said. "Are Americans interested in our ballad literature?" Hutchinson's reply was that he believed Americans read rather more than the same class of people in London. Percy averred that the people read the Scriptures and the law and distorted them both for political purposes. Boswell then made what he hoped would prove a fruitful remark, by stating

[1] See Note 10.

ing that he was curious to know whether a man like Doctor Percy, whose name had become so well known in England since the publication of his "Reliques," was equally esteemed in the Colonies. Earl Percy could have saved the situation by some show of interest in the mention of his clerical protégé; but to Mr. Boswell's infinite chagrin, he began to descant to Hutchinson upon the lack of good literature in American bookshops. He found a sprinkling of the Classics, but nothing in the French language. Beauclerk suggested that, should the cause of the Most Christian King prevail in the impending war, French might soon become the language of America, at which Hutchinson groaned and began to pace up and down the room, his hands clasped behind his back. He recalled the popular jubilation and the solemn observances with which Boston had received the news of the fall of Louisburg and of Wolfe's victory at Quebec. "All this seems but yesterday," he said, "and indeed, it is less than twenty years since we offered up our prayers of thanksgiving to God and pledged our fealty to our King in gratitude that the power of France had been finally crushed. Good God, gentlemen, is it possible that my infatuated countrymen should take to their bosoms the hereditary enemy against whom generations of their ancestors have fought to preserve their birthright? Is Monsieur Vergennes a more promising champion of liberty than Lord North? Has the House of Bourbon shown a greater fondness for the rights of the

the people than the House of Hanover? Surely the times, and the hearts and minds of men, are strangely changed. I feel as if I were in a dream, or the victim of some awful delusion."*

Touched perhaps by Hutchinson's emotion, the company remained silent as he stopped before the fireplace and stretched out his hands to warm them in its genial glow. Then, seating himself in a chair, he leaned forward, gazing into the ruddy light as he had been wont to do when the logs blazed and crackled within the more ample chimney-place of his house on Milton Hill. Paoli was the first to speak. "I have been a rebel, Sir, and I think in a good cause, but the Americans have begun too soon. By that means they will have put themselves back fifty or one hundred years. In another century they will have become a great empire."[1]

"Yes, Sir," said Hutchinson, echoing Paoli's words, "a great empire. I have often thought of that. I have realized what the common increase of population, the growing sense of power, and our great distance from the mother country might in some future age bring to pass. But I have prayed that, when the day of separation came, if come it must, the parting might be like that of a worthy parent and a filial child, where neither gratitude, affection, nor respect should be impaired. God forbid that the land of our fathers should ever have cause to say
of

---

[1] Hutchinson quotes Paoli as having made this remark to him. *Diary and Letters of Thos. Hutchinson*, vol. 1, p. 401.

General James Oglethorpe

Dines Abroad

of us, 'I have nourished children and brought them up, and even they have revolted from me.'"[1]

Sir Joshua took a chair at Hutchinson's side. Mr. Boswell was becoming disturbed. He had failed to command Lord Percy's attention or curiosity, and the evident interest of the company in what Hutchinson had to say was an irritation to his nerves and a menace to his plans. Brooding over his dilemma, he was roused from his thoughts by Beauclerk's assertion that Harry Fox had turned traitor. PERCY. "That is indeed a change of heart and mind. Your authority, Sir." BEAUCLERK. "We have it from the people at Goodwood that he has been writing he has no heart for fighting the Americans and says flatly that they cannot be conquered."[2] OGLETHORPE. "That is hardly treason, I think, Sir." PERCY. "I hope not, General, for I am inclined to agree with Major Fox. I went to America sorely against my will; but when my regiment was ordered away, I could not forget that I was its colonel. Perhaps we might conquer America, but I feel sure that we never shall." HUTCHINSON. "Your Lordship has lost hope? Is that the feeling among military men?" PERCY. "It is rather my own feeling, Sir. We seem unable to make either peace or war. Had Government followed your advice, the Colonies would not have been taxed and, for the time at least, would have abided as the King's obedient and dutiful subjects. Had Mr. Howe pressed home his victories about New York, as

[1] See Note 11.
[2] See Note 12.

as he would have done against French or Spaniards, I think we might have won a peace in 1776. I doubt, though, if the country would have supported the rigorous military measures against the Americans that they would have been quick to applaud if exercised against an alien enemy. I said that we might conquer America, but perhaps it is too late now. The opposition to the war is steadily growing in Parliament. Now we have crossed blades with France. Our fleets and armies are scattered. Burgoyne's misfortune has wrought a mighty change. He has left his army prisoners in New England and is expected home any day.[1] He will not be received with open arms, but I shall be glad to have his views. I fancy he has been more sinned against than sinning." HUTCHINSON. "You have been pleased, my Lord, to commend my public acts. I can never be thankful enough for having been enabled so to conduct myself during the time of my being in Administration that, in all the controversies I have had with the people of the Province, I have never contended in any instance for what I did not think perfectly right, and for the real advantage of the men who were endeavouring my ruin. Without this reflection I could not support myself. I have ever advised against Parliamentary acts for taxing America and have done everything in my power that they might be repealed.* But I cannot be sure that, had my advice been followed, this rebellion could have been averted. Our disputes with the

---

[1] Burgoyne arrived in London May 13, 1778.

the Mother Country about our charters and our rights are of long standing. They date back to another century and have been settled hitherto by prudent compromises. The recent Acts of Parliament placed a weapon in unscrupulous hands; but, lacking these, our demagogues and incendiaries might have found other arguments with which to delude and inflame the people."

Hutchinson was becoming a thorn in the side of Mr. Boswell, but he had his part to play and his perturbation must be concealed. So he inquired if His Excellency thought it altogether unnatural that the Bostonians should have regarded Parliamentary taxation as synonymous with tyranny. HUTCHINSON. "I saw no tyranny in the exercise by Parliament of its undoubted constitutional right. I never could admit a denial of the right of Parliament in all cases, but I wished a forbearance of the Acts of Taxation.* These Acts were not oppressive, but the people were taught to believe that they meant enslavement. The real tyrants in America were not the servants of the Crown." PERCY. "A good friend of yours informed me in Boston that he had rather be governed by one man three thousand miles away than by three thousand men one mile away."[1] HUTCHINSON. "Yes, Sir. His views are quite comprehensible. He had been mobbed."

Mr. Boswell's aversion to Hutchinson increased, but now it was Hutchinson who came to his aid. "I had a call

---

[1] This remark is ascribed to Colonel Ruggles.

call from Doctor Robertson last month," remarked the Governor. "I had never met him, though we corresponded when I was in America. He has lost heart and has laid aside his History of the English Colonies. He gave this reason — that there was no knowing what would be the future condition of them. I told him I thought, be it what it may, it need make no odds in writing the History of what is past, and I thought a true state of them ought to be handed down to posterity." *

The mention of Robertson's name fell upon Boswell's ears like a trumpet call. "Curiously enough, Sir," he exclaimed, "I met Doctor Robertson this morning at the Exhibition, and he was good enough to read the letter to which I have already referred. He commended it highly, and I am sure it will prove of interest to Lord Percy. It is written by Doctor Johnson." "Oh," said Paoli, "Doctor Johnson's letters are always worth reading." The expectant Boswell lifted the letter from the table, only to be foiled by Percy's strange obtuseness and lack of curiosity. "I have not the honour of Doctor Johnson's acquaintance," remarked his Lordship, "but I know the high place he holds in the world of letters, while as a moralist I am informed that he takes higher rank than our good friend Beauclerk here. We have been engaged in a common cause within the year, but our activities did not bring us together. I refer to the case of the unfortunate Doctor Dodd." [1]

At

---

[1] See Note 13.

The Rev. Dr. William Dodd

At another time Boswell would have been eager to hear Percy's story of this famous case, but now he had more serious business in hand. He saw that extreme measures were necessary, the time for finesse had passed, and he addressed this question bluntly to all whom it might concern. "May I read my letter? It is very brief." In an instant he had the attention of every one save Reynolds, who had laid his ear-trumpet across his knees and was opening his snuff-box. No word of Boswell's question had reached Sir Joshua's ear, and all unconscious of the havoc he was making, he remarked to Hutchinson in a somewhat louder tone than usual, "I agree with you, Sir, Robertson is wrong. You are planning, I hope, to continue your History of New England. You will not be deterred by any temporary shiftings of fortune?"

Hutchinson glanced quickly at his host. Paoli's eyes were fixed expectantly upon him, the gaze of all had shifted from the eager Boswell. It was clear that Sir Joshua's question was not to be ignored. With a slight bow in Boswell's direction, Hutchinson replied, "My poor history must be dry and uninteresting except to Americans*— quite uninteresting to the rest of the world. But I am writing now of my own time and of the progress of this Rebellion from its first seed until it arrived at its full growth, not forgetting the watering and manuring from this side."* REYNOLDS. "His Majesty's Opposition have much to answer for. Chatham learned too late that he had been nursing the cause of
men

men whose real intent was the dismemberment of the empire."

The company were now gathering about the fireplace, and Mr. Boswell was desperate. He was certain now that he hated this tall, lank New-Englander in his sober gray attire. Who was he, the discredited governor of a petty province, so to dominate the attention of men of fashion and learning? He groaned inwardly to hear Oglethorpe pressing the interrogation of this obscure person by asking, "Pray, Sir, when shall we have another volume?" HUTCHINSON. "Perhaps not in my lifetime. I am writing of men still living and of issues that are not yet settled." REYNOLDS. "An early publication of your book would be helpful to the cause, it would influence public opinion and Parliamentary action. I believe that the right will prevail." HUTCHINSON. "I know that the Great Governor of the world always does right, and I desire to acknowledge it when I am in adversity as well as in prosperity. I shall never be able to see that there were just grounds for this revolt, and yet the ways of Providence are mysterious, and I abhor the least thought that all is not perfectly right and ordered by infinite rectitude and wisdom." * PAOLI. "Who was the great inspirer of this rebellion?" HUTCHINSON. "A Mr. Adams was rather considered as the opposer of Government, and a sort of Wilkes in New England. He has a great pretended zeal for liberty, and a most inflexible natural temper." *

Boswell

Boswell in his irritation remembered that Wilkes was his friend, and retorted, with some show of asperity, that he should not consider Mr. Wilkes's zeal for liberty as altogether a pretence. HUTCHINSON. "Sir, I doubt his sincerity and dislike his principles. I do not believe they contribute to virtue in government or to the happiness of the governed. I have seen Wilkes but once and that was in Guild hall in 1776. He was accompanied by a mob, as great blackguards as can well be conceived, and they seemed ripe for riot." * REYNOLDS. "At least, you do not stand in fear of mobs here. You are safe without a guard." HUTCHINSON. "I had no guard at home. I depended, Sir, on the protection of Heaven. My principles in government I never concealed, but I was not conscious of having done anything of which they could justly complain or make a pretence for offering violence to my person. I was not sure, but I hoped they only meant to intimidate. By discovering that I was afraid, I should encourage them to go on. By taking measures for my security, I should expose myself to calumny and being censured as designing to render them odious for what they never intended to do." * PERCY. "The New-Englanders are a damnably hypocritical, contentious people. I suppose you will hardly agree to that sentiment, Sir." HUTCHINSON. "Why, no, my Lord. They are for the most part right-minded, industrious, peace-loving folk. They have been deluded and ensnared by unscrupulous agitators. They are my countrymen; all my

my life I have seen them prosperous and contented, and it pains me to think of the miseries that have been brought upon their heads." PERCY. "They have courage and perseverance, that I will maintain, but they do distort the Scriptures and the law." REYNOLDS. "Why is it, Mr. Hutchinson, that your clergy is so generally opposed to Government? Do they preach that in promoting what they call liberty any immorality or evil may be condoned?" HUTCHINSON. "No, Sir. I have never heard such doctrine from the pulpit, but our Ministers are dependent upon the people, they are elected by the people, who when they are dissatisfied get rid of them." * REYNOLDS. "That seems a dangerous relation. You mean that their political attitude is influenced by the people rather than the reverse?" HUTCHINSON. "In some cases this is doubtless so. Not all of our clergymen are opposed to Government. Doctor Caner, who preached in His Majesty's chapel in Boston, is a friend of Government, but he is of the Episcopal faith. Doctor Byles refused to extol the popular cause in his pulpit, and my old friend Doctor Pemberton is also a devout and loyal clergyman. These men are Dissenters and I fear have fallen on evil times." PERCY, smiling. "I hope that no misfortune has come to my friend Doctor Byles. He was the most witty and delightful of companions. He told me, Governor, that you were accused of advocating the rule of the many by the few and that you aspired to be the leader of that chosen few." HUTCHIN-
SON.

son. "I think he was quoting Mr. Adams in that.[1] The statement does no serious violence to my political views, but misrepresents my personal ambitions and desires. I opposed the distortion of the functions of the Town Meeting, a most useful institution in itself, and its conversion into a supreme assembly composed largely of the inferior and even vicious sort of people who paid no regard to the qualifications of voters. These assemblies begot lawlessness and violence. They overrode all law and were sustained by the violence they had incited. For myself, while ever appreciative of His Majesty's confidence and favour, I prayed for relief from administrative duties, as my constitution was not strong enough to cope with the problems and disorders of the time."*

As Hutchinson rose from his chair a smile overspread his pale, thin face. He hoped he would not be regarded as a doleful guest, and voiced Mr. Boswell's sentiments by asserting that he was monopolizing too much of the time of that good company. "I hear it whispered," he continued, "that the American exiles are becoming troublesome, that we grumble intolerably. I hope the charge is not true; at all events, I should be the blackest of ingrates to let the accusation lie against me. My estates in America have been seized, but I am not penniless, and His Majesty's bounty has removed me from any dread

---

[1] Samuel Adams to Stephen Sayre, Nov. 23, 1770. Printed in Frothingham's *Life of Warren*, p. 159.

dread of want. My old friends are scattered, but many of them are my neighbours in this friendly city, and I have my family about me. I have had my public trials and my private griefs, but there is more cause for thankfulness than for repining." PAOLI. "London is a pleasant refuge for the exile. You find here sympathy and good fellowship." HUTCHINSON. "I have met with kindness and consideration on every hand. Some of my friends are taking up their lives here with light hearts, rejoicing in their release from the contentions and violence that disturbed their peace at home; but I have more of the old Athenians in me, and though I know not how to reason upon it, I feel a fondness to lay my bones in my native soil.* I am an American, and I suppose it is the Puritan that speaks in my blood. When I first came to London, I saw Garrick in one of Farquhar's plays and went away unimpressed. I went to Ranelagh and, amid all the light and fashion, was thinking of the more sober parade that in happier days used to throng the mall in my native town. Only the other day, standing in Lord Hardwicke's splendid seat of Wimpole Hall, I thought to myself, this is high life, but I would not have parted with my humble cottage at Milton for the sake of it.* New England is wrote upon my heart in as strong characters as Calais was upon Queen Mary's, but there is this difference: she lost the one by her own folly; I am not sensible I could have kept the other except in a way which would have caused more pain from reflection, than I now feel from the loss of

Thomas Hutchinson

of it.* I have nearly reached my three-score years and ten and I know that you must regard me as old and incorrigible beyond my age."

Percy laid a friendly hand upon Hutchinson's shoulder as he said gaily, " Whatever the issue of this rebellion, I predict that you will soon return to Boston and to the scenes you love. I do not hold the New England people in such contempt as to believe them capable of any prolonged hostility to you. They will remember that what Doctor Robertson has been to Scotland and Mr. Hume to England, you have been to the Massachusetts Bay. Indeed, you have not only written their history, but in your own time have helped to make it honourable by faithful and unselfish service to the State. Political passion will not for long stifle pride in your achievements and party bitterness will give way to gratitude."

"Your praise," said Hutchinson, "is far beyond my deserts, but I do not feel that I have merited the hatred of my countrymen. I wish for their good opinion if it can be acquired without disturbing my peace of mind. I should like to live to see them convinced that I have ever sincerely aimed at their true interest. I have even hoped that I might be instrumental in securing for them every liberty which, as British subjects, they are capable of enjoying."* Then, with an almost whimsical inflection, he added, "I should rather live at Milton than at Kew."*

Percy

Percy smiled. "Then at Milton it shall be. Have I told you of my visit to your home? It was in the fall of 1774. I was driving with Rawdon to the pond at Jamaica Plain. We took the wrong road and found ourselves on Milton Hill. Your son did the honours of the place in a way that would have warmed your heart. A beautiful spot, with its lawns and gardens and that wonderful prospect over sea and land, the river winding through the meadows, the blue expanse of the bay beyond, the wooded hills to the south, and that far-distant mountain peak, near which I think they told me there was a broad township named in your honor."[1] HUTCHINSON. "Most gentlemen from abroad say it has the finest prospect they ever saw, except where great improvements have been made by art, to help the natural view. I hope your Lordship took the longest way, that road being generally equal to the turnpike roads here; the other way is rather rough."* PERCY. "God knows the way we took, for we were lost; but the foliage was ablaze with the autumn colour so peculiar to New England, and we roamed in your garden and among the trees of your planting." HUTCHINSON. "It was a pretty place, Sir — but it has been seized and plundered and my household gods have been scattered to the winds. I am glad it is no longer a barrack."

Lord Percy approached his host, to present his parting compliments. The company gathered about the tall

[1] See Note 14.

tall Corsican, who at this moment became conscious of certain furtive twitchings at the skirts of his coat. He turned his head to meet Boswell's appealing gaze. "Gentlemen," he said, "we have yet to hear Doctor Johnson's letter. I am sure you will gladly spare a moment for any word from him." There was a murmur of assent, and with the company standing grouped about their host, Boswell seated himself at the table, drew a candle toward him, and read as follows:

To JAMES BOSWELL, ESQ.

SIR, — The debate between Doctor Percy and me is one of those foolish controversies which begin upon a question of which neither party cares how it is decided, and which is, nevertheless, continued to acrimony, by the vanity with which every man resists confutation. Doctor Percy's warmth proceeded from a cause which, perhaps, does him more honour than he could have derived from juster criticism. His abhorrence of Pennant proceeded from his opinion that Pennant had wantonly and indecently censured his patron. His anger made him resolve that, for having been once wrong, he never should be right. Pennant has much in his notions that I do not like; but still I think him a very intelligent traveller. If Percy is really offended, I am sorry; for he is a man whom I never knew to offend any one. He is a man very willing to learn, and very able to teach; a man, out of whose company I never go without having learned

learned something. It is sure that he vexes me sometimes, but I am afraid it is by making me feel my own ignorance. So much extension of mind, and so much minute accuracy of inquiry, if you survey your whole circle of acquaintance, you will find so scarce, if you find it at all, that you will value Percy by comparison. Lord Hailes is somewhat like him: but Lord Hailes does not, perhaps, go beyond him in research; and I do not know that he equals him in elegance. Percy's attention to poetry has given grace and splendour to his studies of antiquity. A mere antiquarian is a rugged being.

Upon the whole, you see that what I might say in sport or petulance to him, is very consistent with full conviction of his merit.

I am, dear Sir,
Your most, etc.,
SAM. JOHNSON.[1]

His task discharged, Mr. Boswell mopped his brow, filled and drained his glass. Oglethorpe was heard to murmur, "An excellent letter and most honourable to Doctor Percy." There was a strange expression on Earl Percy's face, something that hovered on the border-line between astonishment and perplexity, as he addressed himself to Boswell. "Do I understand, Sir, that this letter was written by Doctor Johnson to you in the hope that

---

[1] Boswell's *Life*, ed. Hill (1887), vol. 3, p. 277.

An Anecdote of Lord Percy

When his Lordship was leaving Ireland to embark for America with his Regiment he ~~most generously hired~~ (as is well known) most generously hired a Ship ~~to~~ at his own expence to carry over the wives & children of his Soldiers with them to Boston. It happened just as they were ~~embarking~~ going on board that one of the Children was taken ill of the Small Pox, on which his Lordship sent for an eminent Surgeon of Cork, & recommending the Mother & Child to his Care, put into his hands Ten Guineas & with a request to advance whatever further Sums should be wanting for their support, &c. ~~...~~

From a Manuscript in the Handwriting of Dr. Percy

that you would communicate its contents to my friend? It was unsolicited, of course, the product of — what shall we say — a guilty conscience?" Boswell. "It was written in response to a letter of mine, a copy of which I have in my pocket, and should be glad to read if—"[1]

There was a quick gesture of Percy's hand that could not be misunderstood, and Mr. Boswell continued: "I called Doctor Johnson's attention to the injured state of Doctor Percy's feelings, and his letter is characteristic of the tender heart of my illustrious friend, and your Lordship will, I am sure, esteem it as a tribute to Doctor Percy's distinguished merit." Percy. "I do so esteem it. Doctor Percy is worthy of commendation, and I am inclined to esteem all those who value him. At all events, such praise establishes a claim to my regard. I am bound to him by many friendly ties, and during my absence in America he was the most faithful and particular of my correspondents. I suppose that Doctor Johnson's attack was quite unwarranted, but as there was a quarrel, I may hope and assume that my Doctor did not fly the field." Boswell. "Indeed, my Lord, Doctor Johnson felt that he had been treated with great rudeness. I wondered that Doctor Percy should venture as he did." Earl Percy's mood had given place to one of undisguised amusement as he added, "That is well, Sir. I am glad he stood his ground — for the honour of all the Percies!"

Having thus reëstablished the reputation of the author

[1] For Boswell's letter, see *Life*, ed. Hill (1887), vol. 3, p. 277.

thor of the "Reliques" with the House of Northumberland, Boswell, glowing with triumph, became gay and debonair and moved briskly about among the guests. He even smiled complacently upon Hutchinson, and managed to draw Percy aside to express the great happiness it had given him to pass an evening in his company. "I believe," he continued, "that I was not altogether unknown to your Lordship's mother and" — with an appropriate obeisance — "with a fair pride I can boast of the honour of her Grace's correspondence, specimens of which adorn my archives."[1] That half-laughing, half-cynical light which appears in Valentine Green's engraving flashed for an instant in Percy's eyes as with a low bow he turned away.

There was the proper speeding of parting guests, and Earl Percy and the Honourable Topham Beauclerk passed down the stairs together and out into the foggy night. They were in agreement that Paoli had appeared at his best, that Oglethorpe was the soul of perennial youth, that the loss of such men as Hutchinson would make for the undoing of well-ordered civilization in America; and then came the question sharply put in Percy's voice: "Who the deuce is this Mr. Boswell?"

Beauclerk's laughter rang out, and its echoes died away into the melody of belfry clocks chiming the hour. As the young men strolled slowly along to where Percy's coach was standing, they were engaged in warm debate and

---

[1] Boswell's *Life*, ed. Hill (1887), vol. 3, p. 272.

and their language was punctuated by bursts of merriment and frequent repetitions of Boswell's name. "You are wrong, Percy, upon my honour, you are wrong," laughed Beauclerk, as his friend disappeared through the carriage door; and then there came back from the depths of the coach the sound of his Lordship's parting speech: "Now Mercury endue thee with leasing, for thou speakest well of fools."

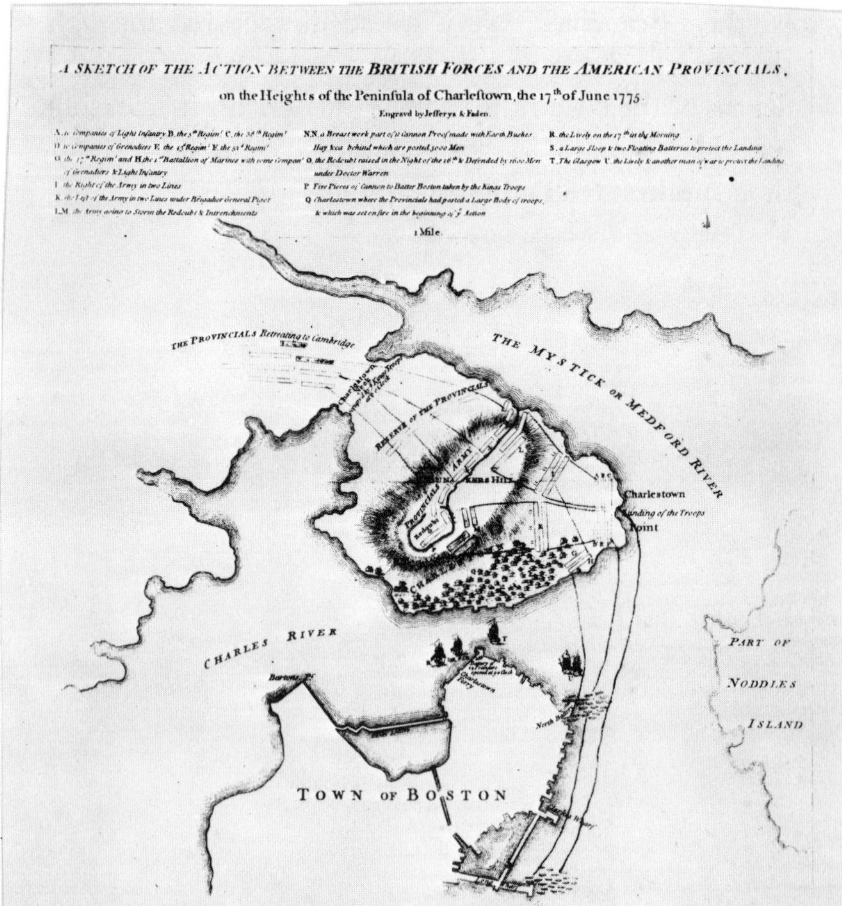
A SKETCH OF THE ACTION BETWEEN THE BRITISH FORCES AND THE AMERICAN PROVINCIALS,
on the Heights of the Peninsula of Charlestown, the 17th of June 1775.
Engravd by Jefferys & Faden.
B. the 5th Regimt. C. the 38th Regimt.
E. the 43d Regimt. F. the 52d Regimt.
H the 1st Battalion of Marines
& Light Infantry
the Right of the Army in two Lines
the Left of the Army in two Lines under Brigadier General Pigot
L.M. the Army going to Storm the Redoubt & Intrenchments
N.N. a Breast work part of it Cannon Proof made with Earth Bushes Hay &ca behind which are posted 5000 Men
O. the Redoubt raised in the Night of the 16th & Defended by 1600 Men under Doctor Warren
P. Five Pieces of Cannon to Batter Boston taken by the Kings Troops
Q. Charlestown where the Provincials had posted a Large Body of troops, & which was set on fire in the beginning of ye Action
R. the Lively on the 17th in the Morning
S. a Large Sloop & two Floating Batteries to protect the Landing
T. The Glasgow V. the Lively & another man of war to protect the Landing
1 Mile.
THE PROVINCIALS Retreating to Cambridge
THE MYSTICK OR MEDFORD RIVER
RESERVE OF THE PROVINCIALS
PROVINCIALS ARMY
BUNKERS HILL
Redoubt
Charlestown
Landing of the Troops
Point
CHARLES RIVER
Charlestown Ferry
North
TOWN OF BOSTON
PART OF NODDLES ISLAND

NOTES

Notes

[1]

TOPHAM BEAUCLERK (1739–1780) was the son of Lord Sidney Beauclerk and so the grandson of the first Duke of St. Alban's and the great-grandson of Charles II and Nell Gwyn, yet he lives in the social and literary annals of his day by virtue of Doctor Johnson's friendship. But for Boswell's narrative, Beauclerk would have been recalled by posterity merely as a discreditable figure in a famous scandal that agitated high life in London more than a century and a half ago, and what Johnson characterized as " his wit and his folly, his acuteness and maliciousness, his merriment and reasoning," would have been lost to the world. Beauclerk was a very accomplished and brilliant gentleman, learned in literature and science, and Boswell assures us that he " was too polite and valued learning and wit too much to offend Johnson by sallies of infidelity and licentiousness." Johnson's admiration for Beauclerk is evidenced in his statement that his " talents were those which he had felt himself more disposed to envy than those of any whom he had known "; and he characterized his conversational qualities in the well-known phrase that " no man ever was so free, when he was going to say a good thing, from a look that expressed it was coming, or, when he had said it, from a look that expressed it had come.'

Lord Bolingbroke had married Lady Diana Spencer, and in March, 1768, he obtained a divorce from her on the ground of adultery with Beauclerk. Two days after the granting of the decree, the offending couple were married at St. George's, Hanover Square. " Lady Di," as she is referred to in the correspondence and memoirs of the time, was a beautiful and gifted woman and made her new husband a faithful and devoted wife. Her artistic talents were highly esteemed in her day, and Horace Walpole was a worshipper at her shrine. The " Beauclerk Closet "

Closet" at Strawberry Hill was set apart for the display of her series of seven designs for Walpole's *Mysterious Mother*.

[2]

Doctor William Pitcairn (1711–1791) was an elder brother of Major John Pitcairn, killed at Bunker Hill. He received his degree of M.D. from Oxford in April, 1749, was elected a Fellow of the College of Physicians in 1750, and was President of that institution from 1775 to 1785. He was elected physician to St. Bartholomew's Hospital in 1750 and resigned in 1780. Four years later he accepted the treasurership of St. Bartholomew's and lived thereafter at the Treasurer's House in the Hospital. He died at his country seat at Islington November 25, 1791. On the death of his brother in America, he took over the care of his fatherless children. The Major's son David (1749–1809) succeeded to Doctor Pitcairn's practice and to many of his honours.

[3]

For an interesting account of this famous relic see *The Gold-Headed Cane*, London, 1828. It was the property successively of Doctors Radcliffe, Mead, and Askew, and by the last-named was bequeathed to Pitcairn. Doctor David Pitcairn succeeded to the ownership on the death of his uncle, and from him the cane passed to Doctor Baillie. It was presented by Baillie's widow to the College of Physicians early in the nineteenth century. The arms of its six distinguished owners are engraved upon the head of the cane.

[4]

General Oglethorpe (1696–1785), founder and patron of the Georgia Colony in America, served under Prince Eugene in his campaign against the Turks in 1716–17. Boswell tells us that, Doctor Johnson having asked him for an account of the siege of Belgrade, the General, "pouring a little wine upon the table, described everything with a wet finger." There is a pleasant characterization of Oglethorpe in Austin Dobson's essay, *A Paladin of Philanthropy*.

Percy's

Notes

[5]

Percy's Brigade, on its return from Lexington on the 19th of April, 1775, entered Charlestown after dark and was ferried across to Boston during the night.

[6]

Henry Pelham was the son of Peter Pelham, the first engraver of mezzotints in America, by his third wife, who was also the mother of John Singleton Copley by a previous marriage. A brotherly affection developed between these young men that continued through life. Copley left Boston in 1774 for an extended tour in Europe and never returned to his native land. Pelham left Boston after the evacuation of the town by the British in 1776 and later joined Copley in London. He died in Ireland in 1806. Pelham's political views are sufficiently indicated by his comments on Joseph Warren, contained in a letter to Susanna Copley:

"I have often passed Doct. Warren's Grave. I felt a disagreeable Sensation thus to see a Townsman an old Acquaintance led by unbounded Ambition to an untimely death and thus early to realise that Ruin which a lust of Power and Dominion has brought upon himself and partly through his means upon this unhappy Country. I would wish to forget his principles to Lament his Fate."

[7]

John Pitt (1756–1835), who succeeded his father as second Earl of Chatham in 1778. He entered the army in 1774, serving on General Carleton's staff in Canada; but, at his father's request, resigned his commission in 1776 to avoid serving against the Americans. On the outbreak of the war with France, he reëntered the military service in 1778, as a lieutenant in the 39th Regiment of Foot, and served throughout the siege of Gibraltar, 1779–83. He attained high rank, but little distinction in the army, and survived his famous brother William by twenty-nine years.

The

Notes

[8]

The following extract from a letter written by a British officer in Boston and printed in the *Detail and Conduct of the War*, is characteristic of the criticism levelled at the British Headquarters after the Battle of Bunker Hill:

"Had we only wanted to drive them from their ground, without the loss of a man, the Cymetry, transport, which drew little water and mounted eighteen nine-pounders, could have been towed up Mystic channel and brought to within musket-shot of their left flank, which was quite naked; and she could have lain, water-borne, at the lowest ebb tide; or, one of our covered boats, musket-proof, carrying a heavy piece of cannon, might have been rowed close in, and one charge on their uncovered flank would have dislodged them in a second.

"Had we intended to have taken the whole rebel army prisoners, we needed only have landed in their rear and occupied the high ground above Bunker's-hill. By this movement we shut them up in the peninsula as in a bag, with their rear exposed to the fire of our cannon, and, if we pleased, our musquetry: in short, they must have surrendered instantly or been blown to pieces."

[9]

It is alleged that the British field artillery was silenced early in the action through having been supplied with over-sized ball for their six-pounders, and that later the guns became mired in the marshes at the foot of Breed's Hill.

The same letter quoted in Note 8 contains the following passage:

"The wretched blunder of the over-sized balls sprung from the dotage of an officer of rank in that Corps, who spends his whole time in dallying with the schoolmaster's daughters. God knows he is old enough — he is no Samson — yet he must have his Delilah."

General Cleveland was the officer referred to, and the ladies, daughters of Master Lovell of the Latin School.

Jonathan

Notes

[10]

Jonathan Trumbull was born April 24, 1750, graduated at Yale in 1767, and died May 10, 1831. The first two cantos of his *McFingal* were published in Philadelphia in 1775, the complete work appearing at Hartford, Connecticut, in 1782.

[11]

This quotation from Isaiah, I, 2, Bishop of London's translation, appears in Hutchinson's hand on a fly-leaf of his *Diary*, accompanied by the words: " Motto for Title-page of a History of the Revolt of the Colonies."

[12]

The Honourable Henry Edward Fox, son of the first Lord Holland, and a younger brother of Charles James Fox. He served as a captain in the 38th Regiment at Bunker Hill, and attained his majority in 1777. For his views on the American War, see letter of Lady Sarah Lennox to Lady Susan O'Brien, dated Goodwood, April 21, 1779, in *Life and Letters of Lady Sarah Lennox*, London, 1901, vol. 1, p. 295.

[13]

Doctor William Dodd, a popular and fashionable preacher, at one time chaplain to George III, was undone by reckless greed and extravagance. In an evil hour, in an effort to save himself from exposure and disgrace, he forged a bond in the name of the Earl of Chesterfield, who had formerly been his pupil. After a trial at the Old Bailey in February, 1777, Dodd was found guilty and condemned to death. Extraordinary efforts were made to secure a pardon. Earl Percy presented a petition for mercy to the King, signed with twenty-three thousand names, while Doctor Johnson employed his pen most generously in behalf of the culprit. London, and indeed all England, was in a ferment over the case during the spring months of 1777, and a whole library of Impartial Accounts,

LIBRARY OF DAVIDSON COLLEGE

Books on regular loan may be checked out for **two weeks**.